Li Y

W9-AJT-440

Stevensville, MI

(269) 429-9575

Developed and produced by Ripley Publishing Ltd

This edition published and distributed by:
Mason Crest Publishers Inc.
370 Reed Road, Broomall, Pennsylvania 19008
(866) MCP-BOOK (toll free)
www.masoncrest.com

Copyright © 2004 by Ripley Entertainment Inc. This edition printed in 2010.
All rights reserved. Ripley's, Believe It or Not!, and Ripley's Believe It or Not!
are registered trademarks of Ripley Entertainment Inc.

Ripley's Believe It or Not!
Life in the Fast Lane
ISBN 978-1-4222-1538-8
Library of Congress Cataloging-in-Publication data is available

Ripley's Believe It or Not!—Complete 16 Title Series
ISBN 978-1-4222-1529-6

No part of this publication may be reproduced in whole or in part, or stored in a retrieval
system, or transmitted in any form or by any means, electronic, mechanical,
photocopying, recording, or otherwise, without written permission from the publishers.
For information regarding permission, write to VP Intellectual Property, Ripley
Entertainment Inc., Suite 188, 7576 Kingspointe Parkway, Orlando, Florida, 32819
email: publishing@ripleys.com

PUBLISHER'S NOTE
While every effort has been made to verify the accuracy of the entries in this book,
the Publishers cannot be held responsible for any errors contained in the work.
They would be glad to receive any information from readers.

WARNING
Some of the stunts and activities in this book are undertaken by experts and should not
be attempted by anyone without adequate training and supervision.

Printed in the United States of America

Believe It or Not!®

LIFE IN THE FAST LANE

Lincoln Township Public Library
2099 W. John Beers Rd.
Stevensville, MI 49127
(269) 429-9575

RIPLEY
PUBLISHING
a Jim Pattison Company

Life In The Fast Lane

Are you crazy about cars? If so, jump on and

enjoy the ride—be dazzled by the Mini Cooper

covered in gold coins, look out for the human

rocket, and keep that stiletto shoe car away

from the monster truck made of balloons;

otherwise we might have a puncture.

*Pyro Boy walks through a
burning ring of fire...*

CoiNinG It!

The mid-1980s MGB Roadster, which is covered in gold-plated English pennies, is currently on display at the Ripley's Museum in Mexico.

YOU COULD SAY that Ken Burkitt of Niagara Falls, Ontario, Canada, is money mad!

Ken's obsession with coins is not confined to his wallet—he has decorated several cars with coins and he spends his time making sure he covers every inch of them. Ken covered this Mini and a limousine with thousands of coins. All of the cars Ken has decorated are in full working order—in fact, they are in mint condition! Each coin that Ken uses is covered with at least eight coats of polyurethane, in order to stop it from discoloring or rusting.

Gold-plated English pennies cover this 1988 Lincoln Continental stretch limousine, part of the Ripley collection.

On most of the cars he decorates, Ken uses coins of various vintages, dating back to the 1860s.

Annie Burkitt

Ken is not the only creative one in the family. His wife, Annie Burkitt, creates portraits of famous people, such as John Lennon, Marilyn Monroe, and Louis Armstrong, from cut lead crystals.

Coins are bent into shape using a vice to make them cover every inch of the car.

Ripley's
COIN-COVERED MINI
EXHIBIT NO: 11647
1969 AUSTIN MINI COVERED IN
GOLD-PLATED ENGLISH PENNIES

Way to Mow!

Gary Hatter of Champaign, Illinois, made a 14,500-mi (23,000-km) journey around America—on a lawnmower! Leaving Portland, Maine, in May 2000, he passed through all 48 continuous U.S. states and dipped into Canada and Mexico, before arriving at Daytona Beach, Florida, in February 2001. One of his proudest moments came halfway through the 260 days of riding when, in Iowa, he overtook another vehicle!

Pole Position

Jenefer Davies Mansfield, a choreographer, staged her *NASCAR Ballet* at a Virginia theater in 2003. The production featured 20 dancers clad in corporate patches of the theater's sponsors. As they leaped around a banked-racetrack stage, occasionally crashing into each other, the dancers were accompanied by the sounds of revving engines. Mansfield hoped to entice NASCAR fans who were in the area for race day.

Tall Order

In 1989, Randall Jones of Georgia built what is believed to be the world's tallest bicycle. It stands at 17 ft 2 in (5 m) tall. The diameter of the front wheel is 26 ft (8 m).

U.S.A.
California

In Blythe, you are not permitted to wear cowboy boots unless you already own at least two cows.

The Car's the Star

Some of the strangest looking vehicles in America can be found at the Art Car Museum in Houston, Texas. Eccentric owners have decorated their cars to reflect their personalities, covering them in everything from buttons and pennies, to grass and flowers. Among the most colorful exhibits are the Roachster, a vehicle decorated like a cockroach; the Swamp Mutha, adorned with birds and curious creatures; Faith, which has a buffalo head at the front of the car; and Rex Rabbit, a car designed in the shape of a huge rabbit.

You Shall Go to the Ball!

Originally a boat that was used to sail the canals of Venice, this wooden Cinderella's carriage has been converted into a roadworthy vehicle—it's even been used as a wedding carriage.

Boy Racer

Robb Lapeen from Flint, Michigan, jumped over nine cars on his motorbike—when he was just eight years old. He has been riding motorbikes since he was two and first raced on ice and dirt at the age of four.

You Win Some...

Dennis L. Wheat, from Malvern, Arkansas, won his car in a raffle. Unluckily for him, however, he later discovered that it was the same car he had traded-in six years earlier!

Supply and Demand

Hyperactive Technologies, a company based in Pittsburgh, currently offers software to fast-food restaurants that predicts customer rushes. The "Hyperactive Bob" system predicts demand using rooftop cameras that monitor traffic entering the eateries' parking lots and drive-thru lanes. By the end of 2005, however, restaurant managers should be able to access software that predicts what customers will actually order—based on the vehicle that they drive.

Crash Test Dummy

A Toronto teenager crashed into six cars as she completed the parking maneuver of her 2001 driving test. She was all set to pass until she turned into the parking lot of the test center, and accidentally pressed the accelerator, hitting the cars.

Emergency Exit

When 41-year-old Fidel Cueva decided to exit a Greyhound bus window, it didn't seem to matter to him that the bus was traveling at 55 mph (90 km/h) through rush-hour traffic. Perhaps it was because he was so upset that the express bus had just bypassed his stop.

Sailing in the Cart

In December 2003, the intrepid Mark McGowan announced that he was planning to sail from London to Glasgow—in a supermarket shopping cart! Attaching a sail to the cart to make use of northerly winds, and with a broom for propulsion and steering, he set off on the maiden voyage of *Ocean Wave II*, hoping to complete the 400-mi (650-km) journey in around nine months. He planned to sing Rod Stewart's "Sailing" every day to keep up his spirits. Alas, after just 65 mi (100 km) he abandoned the voyage because of icy conditions. Undeterred, he embarked on a fresh challenge and pulled a television set through the streets of Milan for 4 mi (6 km)—using a rope tied to his ear.

Mark McGowan in London, on New Year's Eve 2003, at the beginning of his planned trip to Glasgow in a shopping cart.

End of the Line

In 2001, more than 400 New York subway cars were pushed into the sea by a bulldozer off Cape Hanlopen, Delaware. They landed 80 ft (25 m) under the surface of the Atlantic. The aim was to create an artificial reef, attracting more fish.

On the Rocks

The Princess May, which ran aground in 1910 on Sentinel Island, Alaska, during a low tide, rose 30 ft (9 m) in the air! Tugs eventually pulled the vessel from the rocks.

The Bicycle Thief

Ken James of Melbourne, Australia, died when he fell off a bicycle he had stolen. Police found more than 400 stolen bikes at his home.

How Low Can You Go?

Andy Saunders has customized his 1985 Mini in a unique way—by making it the lowest in the world. The mini Mini is just 34 in (86 cm) high.

Full of Hot Air

This monster truck was created by Scottish balloon artist Colin Myles in 2003. Colin has made all sorts of sculptures from balloons, such as a liquorice man, a giant sunflower, and animals including bears and kangaroos.

WINDY CITY

Rock Lobster ·········
The Art Car Weekend, held annually in Houston, Texas, attracts a host of unusual vehicles, including this cute crustacean.

Wheely Slow

A 73-year-old Milwaukee man irked motorists by traveling on the highway at 5 mph (8 km/h)—in his wheelchair. Despite the fact that wheelchairs aren't allowed on the highway, the man took his chances after a transportation service failed to pick him up for his doctor's appointment.

Starting Young

In 2003, after the keys had been left in the ignition of Taccara King's pickup, her two-year-old son started it and crashed it into a transport office at Vero Beach, Florida.

Pedal Power

Grand Prix rules apply in an annual pedal-powered car race. Competitors race around streets in Valentigney, France, with drivers and cars in costume: recent races have seen banana cars with monkey drivers and pumpkin cars with witches at the wheel. The winner is judged on the basis of both speed and costume.

Put Your Foot on the Gas

Roman Kunikov, a Russian professor, has designed gasoline-powered boots. Tests in a public square at Ufa, near Moscow, showed that wearers could achieve speeds of up to 25 mph (40 km/h).

Baling Out

In 2003, in Makoti, North Dakota, John Smith, also known as the "Flying Farmer," jumped his car over 25 bales of hay—covering a total distance of 160 ft (50 m). John had told his wife earlier that year that if he hadn't sold the hay bales by the start of February, he would jump over them in his car.

ON THE MOVE

- Until 1979, the Egyptian driving test consisted of driving 20 ft (6 m) forward and then the same in reverse

- An English woman took 330 driving lessons and 48 tests before finally passing in 1987

- Instead of windshield wipers, drivers of the first cars rubbed potatoes over the glass to help the rainwater run off

- Helen Ireland of Auburn, California, failed her driving test when she drove straight into the wall of the test center

A Barrel of Laughs ···
Speeds of up to 15 mph (25 km/h) can be reached by these wacky racers of beer kegs, in Windsor, England.

High-flyer

Setting the world record for the highest human flight with a rocket belt, American stunt expert Eric Scott reached a height of 152 ft (46 m). He strapped the rocket belt around his waist and, with the aid of the jetpack on his back, took off in the skies over London in 2004.

U.S.A. Indiana

In Gary, a person may not enter a movie house, theater, or ride a public streetcar within four hours of eating garlic.

Sticky Situation

A West Virginia woman was literally glued to the floor, when she didn't realize that the 3M liquid bandage she had applied to her heel had dripped down to her toes. Family members had to call 911, and three paramedics took more than an hour and a bottle of baby oil to free her. The woman said the humiliation of still being in her robe was by far the worst part of the experience.

Hamburger Harley

Harry Sperl rides around Daytona Beach, Florida, with relish—on an 1100 cc Harley-Davidson trike that has been covered with a huge Fiberglass-and-Styrofoam hamburger. The Hamburger Harley comes with a melting-cheese fender and ketchup-bottle shock covers. Harry's love for bikes is matched only by his passion for burgers. He also owns the world's only Hamburger Museum.

Rocket Man

By fitting 24 rockets to his luge, a light toboggan, Billy Copeland of Ashland City, Tennessee, can reach speeds of nearly 100 mph (160 km/h) in just six seconds on steep hills.

Higher Car

Gary Duval of Colton, California, has built a car that measures 10 ft 11 in (3 m) high from the ground to the roof. It sits on eight monster truck tires, has two separate engines, and took more than 4,000 hours to build.

Talking Turkey

Josh Harper overslept on Christmas Day 2002 and had to drive to his girlfriend's house for dinner, so he decided to cook the turkey on his car engine while he traveled the 90 mi (145 km) to her home in Bristol, England. "The potatoes were a little firm," he said, "but the turkey was done to a treat."

Tug of Love

In 2000, 20 men pulled an 18-ton dump truck around a parking lot in Kenosha, Wisconsin, for an hour without stopping. By the end, they had pulled the truck a total distance of 3¹/₃ mi (5 km).

Toilet Roll

In 1999, Hank Harp drove a motorized toilet the length of Britain—a total of 874 mi (1,300 km). He sat on the seat of the chemical toilet, which was powered by an electric motor and had a top speed of 4 mph (6 km/h), and stored the supplies that he needed for his journey in the bowl.

On his Knees
Australian charity worker Suresh Joachim attempted to break the world record for a continuous crawl in 2001. The current record, which was set in 1992, stands at 31 1/3 mi (50.5 km). To break this, Joachim needed to complete 2,500 laps of his enclosure on the streets of Sydney, Australia.

Milking it

Sam Draper and Julie Magenis of Houston, Texas, have turned a 1979 Cadillac into the Cow-de-lac. Painted black and white like a Friesian cow, the car has an Astroturf interior and upholstery made from feed and potato sacks. The hood is adorned with model cows while the roof displays a farmyard scene.

Revving up

English vicar Rev. Paul Sinclair, also known as the "Faster Pastor," has a sidecar hearse on his motorcycle so that he can give deceased bikers a suitable send-off. It cost £30,000 ($44,500) to convert his 955 cc machine, which can hold a coffin at speeds of up to 70 mph (115 km/h).

Jump to it

Texan parachutist Mike Zang managed to jump out of a plane 500 times in less than 24 hours over Fort Worth, Texas, in May 2001. This means he achieved an average of one parachute jump every three minutes, despite mechanical problems, lightning, and heavy rain.

Ripley's®
STICK ROLLS ROYCE
EXHIBIT NO: **13081**
TOOK 4,609 HOURS TO COMPLETE, AND MEASURES 12 FT 8 IN (4 M) IN LENGTH

Match That
More than 1 million matchsticks went into the construction of this Rolls-Royce, made by Englishman Reg Pollard in 1987. He used the most matchsticks ever recorded in one model—1,016,711!

Pulling Power
In 1990, bodybuilder Georges Christen decided to test his pulling power by holding on to ropes attached to three light aircraft as they attempted to take off.

Not in my Backyard
Back in 1969, when he was still studying at high school, Kim Pedersen made the initial sketches of a monorail he wanted to build in his backyard. Unsurprisingly, his parents dismissed the whole idea, but now that Kim has a place of his own, he has finally been able to realize his dream. Consequently, his home in Fremont, California, is probably the only one in the world with a working monorail in the backyard. The track runs 300 ft (90 m) around the perimeter of his backyard and is 8 ft (2.4 m) tall at its highest point. The monorail took five years to construct, at a cost of $4,000, but monorail-mad Kim thinks it's worth every cent!

The Fastest Milkman in the West
Welsh racing-driver Richard Rozhon established the inaugural world speed record for the electric milk-float. He managed to get the humble machine to accumulate 73 mph (117 km/h) at a milk-float speed trial in Leicestershire, England, in 2003.

Way to Go
The Appian Way, which originally connected Rome, Italy, with Capua, was so well built that it is still in use after more than 2,000 years. The 4-ft (1-m) thick highway, which is more than 350 mi (550 km) long, would cost more than $500,000 a mile to build today.

The Jet Set
The latest pastime for thrill-seeking adrenalin junkies on the Caribbean island of St. Marten is to stand on the beach at the end of the runway at Princess Juliana International Airport and try to remain upright as the huge airplanes take off. People have been tossed in the air by the sheer force of the planes flying so low overhead.

First-class Lounge
As a nine-year-old boy, Gregory Langley always flew first-class—because he had a seat from his favorite plane, Concorde, installed in his home.

DestiNed for *GREAT* Heights

AT TEN YEARS old Paul Hill could have been the world's youngest pilot, and he was certainly the youngest boy in England ever to fly a plane.

Paul's dream to fly Concorde may not have come true, but he was delighted with his successful take-offs and landings.

Paul successfully flew a Cessna 150—with a qualified co-pilot.

After watching his father, Terry, take flying lessons, Paul soon picked up the necessary skills, although he couldn't fly solo until he turned 17.

Tanks Very Much

An Austrian soldier was fined for speeding… in a 25-ton tank. Even though he was on a military exercise, the soldier had to pay the fine for driving at 40 mph (60 km/h) within a 30 mph (50 km/h) zone.

Take the Long Way Home

A luxury limousine that contains a king-sized waterbed—and even a swimming pool—holds the record as the longest car ever built. The 1980 Cadillac stretches to 100 ft (30 m) long and has 26 wheels.

Blind Faith

Scott Duncan and Pamela Habek set off from their home city of San Francisco in October 2004 in a bid to sail around the world alone—even though they are both legally blind. They are relying on electronic aids to navigate their 32-ft (10-m) cutter, Tournesol, on a unique voyage that is expected to take two years.

Starring Rolls

Graham Crossley of Sheffield, England, is crazy about Rolls-Royces—even though he can't drive. The 41-year-old has been in love with Rollers since the age of 11. He has a collection of more than 2,500 photographs, tours garages, and often spends his weekends washing other people's Rolls-Royces for nothing—just so that he can get close to his favorite cars.

Making a Splash

In 1998, Frenchman Alain Vagh created a ceramic-tiled bath to his own specifications—nothing unusual about that, except that it was installed in the back of his Jeep! Now his kids can splash about as much as they like while bathing on the open road.

Sign of the Times

Confused by a Los Angeles freeway sign, artist Richard Ankrom took matters into his own hands in 2001. He scaled the sign and added a vital direction so well that state officials were unable to detect the alteration. After tracking down the authentic reflective buttons that make up each letter from a company in Tacoma, Washington, he added the helpful word "north" to the sign. While making the change, he wore a hard hat and orange fluorescent vest to avert suspicion.

Beer Necessities

Police in Grand Island, Nebraska, reported that after a heavy snowstorm in 2001, a man stole a snowplow from a Hastings storage shed and drove it 20 mi (30 km)—just to buy a case of beer.

Going Flat Out

In 1995, Dutch cyclist Fred Rompelberg achieved the highest ever recorded speed on a bicycle—more than 167 mph (269 km/h) —at Bonneville Salt Flats, Utah.

Space Race

The crew of the command module *Apollo 10* became the fastest human beings ever when the module reached 24,791 mph (39,900 km/h).

Self-build

Measuring 19 ft 4 in (6 m) in length and weighing 2,800 lb (1,270 kg), this Longhorn V-12 took Texan Oliver Albert 12 years to build—by hand! Oliver built it using the best parts of more than 14 different types of vehicle—including a Cadillac, Chevrolet, Chrysler, Dodge, Ford, Jeep, Lincoln, Mercedes, Mercury, Nash, Plymouth, Pontiac, Renault, and Terraplane.

Breaking Step

The San Francisco Bay to Breakers foot race attracts up to 75,000 runners, many of them in a variety of costumes such as giant chickens, Batman, and sets of dominoes.

In the Name of the Lawn

The National Lawnmower Racing Championships take place in Mendota, Illinois. The race started out as an April Fools' joke in 1992, but has proved so popular that it has become an annual event.

Head Over Heels

This giant stiletto was built in the Philippines around a 1,000 cc Japanese motorbike.

Keeping his Cool

In February 2000, actor Paul Newman became the world's oldest racing driver when he competed at the Daytona International Speedway in Florida. He was 75 years and 11 days old on the day—and his co-driver was just 17.

FLIGHT PLAN

- At any time of day, more than 60,000 people are airborne over the U.S.A.

- The wingspan of a Boeing 747 is longer than the Wright brothers' maiden flight

- Chicago's O'Hare International Airport is the world's busiest. An airplane takes off or lands every 37 seconds

- The first female flight attendants were required to weigh no more than 115 lb (52 kg), to be trained nurses, and to be unmarried!

You Wanna Jet?

Andy Green reached an amazing 763 mph (1,228 km/h) in *Thrust*, his twin-jet-engine, supersonic car in October 1997. He established a world land-speed record at the event in the Black Rock Desert, Nevada.

Another Fine Mess

A massive speeding fine of more than $200,000 was issued to millionaire Jussi Salonoja in Finland in 2004. The amount was calculated to reflect Mr. Salonoja's large income.

From the Bottom to ZZ Top

Depicting many world-famous musicians—including ZZ Top, Madonna, Jimi Hendrix, and Sir Elton John—the creators intended to purvey the message "music lives forever." The car is decorated with sculpted styrofoam, and covered with beads, glass, jewelry, and albums.

"GRATEFUL UNDEAD" EXHIBIT NO: 21480
CREATED BY HOUSTON ART TEACHER
REBECCA BASS AND 19 ART STUDENTS

Reach for the Skies

The annual run up the Empire State Building has imitators all over the world, including a run up the monumental Petronas Towers in Malaysia.

Table Mountain

The Annual Furniture Race in Whitefish, Montana, involves competitors attaching skis to various items of furniture and racing down the nearby Big Mountain.

Pump up the Volume

A never-to-be-forgotten family reunion of 55 members—aged from three to 37—was organized by Roger Dumas. Dumas labored for more than 20 years to build a bicycle that could hold them all! During the construction process, he used parts from 150 other bicycles, but Dumas claimed that the vehicle was built entirely without plans.

It's a Knockout

In November 2004, Romanian Alin Popescu stole a car and then crashed into a tree and knocked himself out after traveling half a mile. He was lucky not to have been killed, especially as he is blind.

Going on a Bender

Uri Geller became famous as a spoon-bending psychic. His art car, called "The Geller Effect," is a Cadillac completely covered with thousands of pieces of bent cutlery.

Galloping Gourmets

The 26-mi (40-km) course of *Le Marathon du Cahors et de la Gastronomie* in France is dotted with feeding stations serving foie gras paté, truffles, and copious quantities of wine. Most competitors are in fancy dress, and the race is followed by a wine festival.

Canada

In Alberta, if you are released from prison, it is required that you are given a handgun with bullets and a horse, so you can ride out of town.

One Careful Owner

Retired science teacher Irvin Gordon of East Patchogue, New York, drives a 1966 Volvo P1800S that has well over 2 million mi (3 million km) on the clock—the highest mileage recorded by any car in the world. Irvin has been the car's only owner—he bought it new in June 1966. He used to commute 125 mi (200 km) to work every day, and loves his car so much that since he retired he often drives to other states for lunch.

Engine Room

Two production cars that were built in the early 20th century hold the record for the largest engine capacity. The Peerless 6-60, which was built between 1912 and 1914, and the Fageol, which was built in 1918, both had 13.5-liter engines.

Dead Heat

Manitou Springs, Colorado, is famous for its annual coffin races, in which competitors zoom down the town's main street in wheeled coffins.

Recycled Cycles

In the 1930s, Joseph Steinlauf, a mechanic from Chicago, Illinois, created bicycles made from all sorts of material, including guns, a sewing machine, and even an old headboard and a hot-water bottle! The gun bicycle weighed about 350 lb (160 kg).

Wheel of Fire

KNOWN AS "PYRO BOY," website designer Wally Glenn's life is a hotbed of flames!

Wally Glenn walks through rings of flames, wearing a fire-retardant suit, and with explosives strapped to his body. At a death-defying event at Ripley's Aquarium in Myrtle Beach, South Carolina, in November 1999, Pyro Boy braved temperatures as high as 2,000°F (1,100°C).

Pyro Boy designed his own helmet and outfit, which were made from fire-retardant material.

Once inside the suit, Pyro Boy had 20 lb (9 kg) of explosives strapped to his body.

Pyro Boy bravely walks through rings of fire. He did it once and was unharmed, but another time he caught fire!

The event was more than just a flash in the pan: It was recorded for the Ripley television show in November 1999 at Ripley's Aquarium in Myrtle Beach, South Carolina.

With temperatures reaching as high as 2,000°F (1,100°C) outside the suit, it's no surprise that Pyro Boy's neck was singed beneath his suit.

21

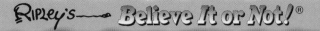

He Sure Can Carry a Note

J. Clark Cullom, of Cincinnati, Ohio, carried a piano with him wherever he went! He traveled more than 15,000 mi (24,000 km) with it strapped to his car.

Hitting the Roof

A Massachusetts man was getting ready for his Fourth of July cookout when the fireworks started early: a Ford Taurus drove off an elevated parking lot and crashed through the roof of his house. No one was hurt in the freak accident, but guests were surprised to see the car sticking out of the roof when they arrived to begin the celebrations.

Good Day at the Office, Dear?

Swapping desks was taken to new extremes when Edd China invented the world's first "office car." The roadworthy workspace made its debut in London, England, in 2003, at the start of a 900-mi (1,500-km) charity road trip to the South of France.

Boom or Bust

Dannie Eaves, an employee at an Oregon bronze shop, was pulled over by police because of six busts in his pickup truck. Dismayed motorists mistook the sculptures for dead bodies and called the cops.

A Dream Wedding

A bride's dream of a memorable wedding came true when she arrived at the ceremony in a four-poster bed on wheels. Lisa Turner followed groom Simon Croft, who traveled in a mobile office, complete with boardroom table and water cooler, in a bizarre 5-mi (8-km) procession in Hampshire, England, in 2004.

DRIVE DOWN YOUR 'TOTAL' OFFICE COSTS

with beoffices.com

H116 HDY

U.S.A.
Kansas

In Wichita, before proceeding through the intersection of Douglas and Broadway, motorists must get out of their vehicle and fire three shotgun rounds into the air.

Bouncing Babies

In a freak accident, two young toddlers fell three stories from a Los Angeles apartment window—and lived. The resilient toddlers were taken to the hospital to be checked out, but soon recovered.

Dead Man Walking

Despite the fact that his family thought he'd been hit by a train, Dane Squires of Toronto was very much alive—and in the dark about arrangements for his funeral service. He called his daughter's cell phone just as his casket was being loaded into a hearse, causing her to freak out, believing his ghost was trying to contact her. The man's sister had previously identified the dead body to be his.

Blind Ambition

Being blind hasn't stopped Mike Newman setting speed records. He set the first world record for unsighted driving on a motorbike at 89 mph (143 km/h) in 2001. Then, in 2003, he broke the record for unsighted driving when he reached 144 mph (232 km/h) in a Jaguar XJR.

All Aboard!

All 34 members of India's Army Services Corps Tornadoes go for a spin on an Indian-built Enfield Bullet 500 cc motorcycle in Bangalore in June 2004.

Wheels on Fire

Roller-blading was no easy task back in 1906. Inventor Alphonse Constantini invented motor-driven skates—they could travel at up to 40 mph (64 km/h).

Wind Tunnel

Slow riders in the Netherlands needn't worry—there is an 8-mi (13-km) long tunnel that contains massive electric fans—they push along riders at up to 28 mph (45 km/h).

Bag of Tricks

Indian magician O.P. Sharma drives a motorbike as part of a stunt, with a black bag over his head in August 2004—and it wasn't on an empty road, but a busy street in the city of Patna.

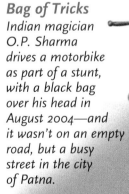

A Fishy Business

If you ask Singapore businessman Lawrence Ng what's in the tank of his Jaguar, the answer is simple: Fish. By ripping out the seats and engine, and sealing the windows and doors, he has converted his car into a big fish tank. The trunk and hood are home to filter systems and air pumps, and the fish are fed through the sunroof.

New York Minute

It has been calculated that people in New York travel, on average, a farther distance vertically than they do horizontally. This is due to the height of the many tall buildings, which makes it necessary to climb more than walk on the level.

Wheely Fast

The fastest speed ever achieved on a motorcycle is 322 mph (518 km/h). Dave Campos set the record at Bonneville Salt Flats, Utah, in 1990.

Crash Course

A truck driver deliberately crashed his truck into a parked car outside a bank in Olhsdorf, Austria, thinking it was a getaway vehicle. It wasn't, and the truck driver was liable for repairs and a hefty fine.

The Sky's the Limit

The new Airbus A380 will be the world's largest aircraft when it comes into service in 2007. Its wingspan is nearly 262 ft (80 m), and it stands 80 ft (25 m) tall. The plane will be fitted with casinos, bars, and even gyms for its 555 passengers.

Around the World in 39 Days

Mohammed Salahuddin Choudhury and his wife Neena of Calcutta, India, circumnavigated the Earth by car in just 39 days. They completed their record-breaking journey in Delhi in 1991.

Close Encounters

In 1996, Nevada State Route 375 was officially named the "Extraterrestrial Highway" by the Nevada Governor, Bob Miller. The highway is, apparently, one of the most "visited" in the country.

Monster Mash

"Bigfoot" is the biggest monster truck in the world: it is 15 ft 5 in (4.7 m) tall, weighs 38,000 lb (17,000 kg) and has 10-ft (3-m) high tires. It was made by Bob Chandler of St. Louis, Missouri.

A Real Hummer-dinger
It's 39 ft (12 m) long, 8½ ft (2.5 m) wide, and it costs $1,500 (£1,000) a night to hire—it's Britain's longest stretch limousine, a Hummer, owned by Scott Demarel of Bristol.

Arriving in Style
Inside, chilled drinks on tap, luxurious leather seating, and air-conditioning make bumpy rides a thing of the past.

My Hands Are Tied

In 2004, Italian Alberto Cristini swam the 2 mi (3 km) from the island of Alcatraz to San Francisco in 1 hour, 50 minutes—with his hands and feet tied together! Fighting strong currents, Alberto, who lives near Venice, made it through the freezing cold stretch of water. The race was pioneered in 1955 by fitness guru Jack La Lanne, who did it while wearing handcuffs.

Plane Stupid

Louis Kadlecek had never flown a plane, but stole a two-seater Cessna from an airport in Houston, Texas, and flew for about a mile before crashing into electricity lines. Mr. Kadlecek was unhurt and walked home after the accident, before being arrested by police.

Just Deserts

The Baja 1,000 Desert Race takes place every November. It's a famous test of endurance, during which car drivers have been known to cover the very bumpy 1,000-mi (1,500-km) course with broken bones. Ivan "Ironman" Stewart completed the course in just 20 hours in 1998.

The Flip Side

At the Gravity Games in Rhode Island, in 2002, Carey Hart performed a back flip on a motorcycle, traveling 20 ft (6 m) before landing. It was the first recorded back flip on a full-size bike.

Judge Dread

Officials in Mount Holly, New Jersey, decided to introduce humorous road signs because the conventional kind were not proving to be effective enough. The colorful signs bear messages such as "Meet Our Judge—Exceed 25 mph (40 km/h)" and "Free Speeding Tickets Ahead."

Chuting Star

In his lifetime, Henry ("Cloudbuster Hen") Langer ascended in an aircraft 479 times but never once landed in a plane—instead, he parachuted back to Earth every time.

U.S.A.
New York

Citizens may not greet each other by "putting one's thumb to the nose and wiggling the fingers."

Motor Boat
In 1999, a rather unusual vehicle was licensed to travel on the roads. Englishman John Brown customized his Robin Reliant car and a Mombar speedboat. Now the road-legal watercraft doesn't have to stop at Land's End!

Oar-inspiring
Measuring 140 ft (42 m) and weighing 2,200 lb (1,000 kg), the world's longest rowing boat requires 24 rowers.

Jam Session
In 1864, in order to get to work in Pueblo, Colorado, school teacher Clara Weston waded across the Arkansas River twice a day for four months.

Putting a Spoke in her Wheels
In 2004, police who were raiding the home of a woman in Berlin, Germany, found no fewer than 78 stolen bicycles stacked in high piles.

The Good Ship Lollipop
In 2003, Robert McDonald from Emmeloord, Holland, stayed afloat for 19 minutes on a boat made out of 370,000 lollipop sticks. The experience has inspired him to plan the construction of a 50-ft (15-m) replica Viking longship made from 15 million lollipop sticks, in which he one day hopes to sail across the Atlantic.

Life Ups and Downs

WHEN RICHARD RODRIQUEZ began his attempt to break the world record for riding on a roller coaster, he had no idea he would take 2,000 rides during the year 2000!

Bumpy Ride
Al McKee covered 45,000 mi (67,500 km) during 60,000 trips on one roller coaster—he was the driver of the scenic railway ride at New Jersey's Palisades Amusement Park.

The university lecturer from Chicago, Illinois, performed all 2,000 rides on the same Big Dipper in Blackpool, England, and timed each ride to see how fast he could go. When asked what he did to pass the time while on the Big Dipper, he said he sent text messages and read books and newspapers.

In his latest attempt to break a record, Richard Rodriguez has so far spent a quarter of a year on a roller coaster!

Cheap Thrills

John Ivers of Bruceville, Indiana, likes roller coasters so much that he has built one in his backyard. Blue Flash, the 180-ft (55-m) long, 20-ft (6-m) high ride, wraps round his barn and a tree. It cost just $1,500 and has a top speed of 25 mph (40 km/h).

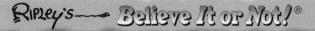
Golden Wedding

When the Sultan of Brunei's son got married in September 2004, the wedding car was a $20 million, gold-encrusted stretch Rolls-Royce. The luxury car was open-topped to accommodate a double throne for Crown Prince Al-Muhtadee Billah Bolkiah and his bride Sarah Salleh. Since even money couldn't buy perfect weather, a golden umbrella was fitted to the car to protect the couple from the rain.

U.S.A.
New York

While riding in an elevator, it is illegal for one to talk to another, or to fold one's hands while looking toward the door.

Race Relations

The island of Tobago hosts annual goat and crab races. Goat jockeys run around the race track alongside the goats, while the crabs are harnessed with string and encouraged along their course by prods from their jockeys.

Pajama Party

Every January, American bed-racing enthusiasts flock to Arizona for the annual Oatman Bed Race. Following a nightwear parade, the teams push their beds down the main street, make their beds, and then race back to the finish line… all to the sweet sounds of the Chamber Pot Band. Even burly bikers have been known to swap their leathers for fluffy pajamas.

Elementary, My Dear Watson

Lloyd Scott, a former British soccer player, used a big-wheeled penny farthing bicycle to cross the continent of Australia in the fall 2004. Scott's 2,700-mi (4,500-km) ride from Perth to Sydney—dressed as Sherlock Holmes—was estimated to have raised almost $2.7 million for charity.

He Swims Like a Fish

Brazilian Jose Martins Ribeiro Nunes, who is also known as "Ze Peixe" or "the fish," is 74 years old and leads an exceptionally active life—he guides ships in and out of Brazil's port by swimming along in front of them. He often swims about 8 mi (12 km), in extremely choppy waters, to guide the vessels safely into and out of the harbor! Jose's lifestyle has made him famous on land and at sea, all over the world.

On Home Ground

A river steamer that ran aground off Sauries Island, near Portland, Oregon, was turned into a houseboat.

Tanks a Million

On his 265-acre (107-ha) estate, Texas millionaire David Estes used to use 25 military tanks to teach corporate employees leadership through his company, Tactical Tanks. One important lesson participants learned was about communication, because Estes intentionally created chaos, disinformation, and ambiguity in the activities to test them.

Pay Day

It took decades, but an Arizona man has finally paid a $1 parking ticket 38 years after he received it. He found the ticket in an old box that he'd carted around through moves in more than six states and decided it was high time to pay up.

All the Fun of the Fair

Max Tate of Newcastle, England, has converted a fairground bumper car into a street-legal vehicle capable of speeds of 90 mph (145 km/h).

Shoe Tree

On Highway 50 near Middle Gate, Nevada, a lone cottonwood tree is draped with hundreds of pairs of shoes thrown over the branches by passers-by. The first pair are said to have been tossed there during a wedding-night row between young newlyweds.

Slow Coaches

A group of high school seniors from Indiana drove so slowly in traffic—at approximately 15 mph (25 km/h)—as a prank, that police cited them for reckless driving. The officers were miffed because the students' low speeds caused a 60-car back-up on an Indiana freeway that took them 20 minutes to clear up.

Going Like a Rocket

Billy Copeland rode his rocket-powered skateboard at 70 mph (113 km/h) in 1998, setting a world record.

U.S.A.
North Dakota

In Fargo, one may be jailed for wearing a hat while dancing, or even for wearing a hat to a function where dancing is taking place.

Carted Around

Andy Tyler of Suffolk, England, has created the world's fastest shopping cart—by fitting it with a jet engine! Powered by gas and liquid fuel, it can reach speeds of over 50 mph (80 km/h). There are drawbacks. In order to propel the cart, the engine explodes 40 times a second and is so noisy that it hurts Andy's ears—and he's unlikely ever to be allowed to take it round his local supermarket!

Moving Home

This brick house in Palm Beach, Florida, was donated to a children's charity and moved in one piece to its new location by truck and by barge.

Hair-raising

Entrepreneur Pat Nevin has just the thing for kids to give their parents a shock—his "Hairy Helmets" are colored mohawks that he velcros on to bicycle helmets. He hopes Harley riders might like to try his styles too.

Baby You Can Drive My Car

According to a car survey by Yahoo!Autos, U.S. freeways may be a better place to meet people than weddings or bars, as 62 per cent admitted that they love to flirt behind the wheel—and that they are more attracted to those who drive nicer cars.

Holy Roller

In the 1970s, it was not unusual to see this mobile church on Britain's roads. The brainchild of one Rev. Dunlop, it was an ordinary bus that was painted to look like a church, complete with a spire sticking out of the roof.

Disco to Go

Anyone hailing a taxi in Aspen, Colorado, could be in for an unusual journey. Jon Barnes' Ultimate Taxi offers a ride complete with disco ball, smoke machine, strobe lights, lasers, and a dry-ice machine. As if that weren't enough, there's even a drum kit, keyboard, and a gift shop in the trunk.

We Have Lift Off!

The SpaceShipOne team members launched themselves into the record books with their successful private space flight.

ON OCTOBER 4, 2004, SpaceShipOne rocketed into history, becoming the first private, manned spacecraft to exceed an altitude of 328,000 ft (100,000 m)!

In doing so—twice within a two-week period—team members claimed the $10 million Ansari X Prize in an international competition designed to spur civilian spaceflight. The competition included seven teams from the U.S.A., as well as groups from Argentina, Canada, Romania, the U.K., and Russia.

Seeing Stars

The fastest-ever spacecraft were two German probes. They were launched from Cape Canaveral, in Florida, and reached 158,000 mph (254,280 km/h) during their orbit of the Sun.

Couch Potatoes
It may look like any old sofa, but this one can reach speeds of up to 87 mph (140 km/h)! Licensed for use on U.K. roads, it was created by inventors Edd China and David Davenport, and is powered by a 1300 cc engine. The steering-wheel is made out of a medium-sized pizza pan and the brake pedal is a cola can.

Put Your Foot in It
A veteran skydiver got his foot caught outside an airplane door and it dangled there in the Pittsburgh skies for 30 minutes. He was still hanging upon landing, but wasn't hurt.

In the Pink
Janette Benson of Macclesfield, England, paid $15,000 (£10,000) to have her Mini Cooper customized—just so that it matched her $30 (£20) handbag! She wanted the new car to be an exact match for her pink bag and splashed out the extra cash for the pink finish and trim.

Hubble, Bubble...
Heavy rains in August 2004 created a bubblefest in Dunn, North Carolina, thanks to soap-based run-off from a factory. A 20-ft (6-m) tall wall of white bubbles obscured the road, but some drivers tried to navigate the mess. Smart ones waited until local firefighters tamed the foam with their hoses.

Chainsaws Massacred
This unusual stretch motorbike is powered by 24 chainsaws.

Power Napping
Englishman Edd China specializes in weird vehicles. For $150 (£100), he takes tourists around London on a motorized four-poster bed. The bed, welded to a 1,600 cc Volkswagen engine, has insurance, and all legal road-testing, and was inspired by the 1960s TV series *The Monkees.* "It cost $7,500 (£5,000) and took two months to build," says Edd, "but it impresses the women!" He also drives a bathtub and a motorized sofa.

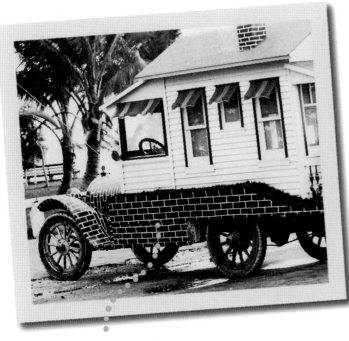

Tough Luck

A 17-year-old teenager from Washington survived a car crash that left her trapped down a ravine in her car for eight days. Doctors think that dehydration may have saved her life, as it stopped a blood clot in her brain from expanding. She was found by an acquaintance, who said she felt led to the site by a dream.

Going Solo

The world's smallest street-legal car was produced on Britain's Isle of Man in the 1960s. The Peel P50 was 53 in (135 cm) high, 53 in (135 cm) long, and 39 in (100 cm) wide. It carried one adult and could reach a top speed of 40 mph (65 km/h).

Home Away from Home

Charles Miller of Portland, Oregon, created domestic bliss in the back of his truck. The vehicle he made home was 3 ft 9 in (1.2 m) wide and 6 ft (1.8 m) long, and he toured the country clocking up more than 200,000 mi (300,000 km) on the way.

High Jinx

Certain street signs in Eugene, Oregon, routinely get stolen by students attending the University of Oregon as decoration for their rooms. The sign for High Street has been replaced nearly 350 times in the last decade, and the city has spent at least $50,000 on new signs in the last year alone.

Learner Driver

An 11-year-old Kansas City boy, who had previously driven only a tractor, took off on a 200-mi (320-km) trip in the family car after being involved in an argument at his school. At one point he ran out of gas, but some construction workers helped him to refuel. However, his big adventure finally stalled when he locked himself out of the car after taking a break. His parents sent him straight back to school the very next day.

In Distress

After an Oregon man's television began emitting the international distress signal (the 121.5 megahertz beep emitted by crashed airplanes and sinking boats), the Air Force, a county search-and-rescue deputy, and the police arrived at his door. The distress signal had been picked up by a satellite, relayed to an Air Force base in Virginia, on to the Civil Air Patrol, and finally to officials in Oregon. The man hurried to replace his TV as he didn't want to pay a $10,000 daily fine should his old set pipe up again.

Drinking and Driving

In 2003, Tony Anchors, from Didcot, England, wanted to do something completely different with his Mini—so he converted it into a mobile bar!

InDex

ACKNOWLEDGMENTS

Jacket (b/r) Northscot Press Agency/Rex Features

9 (b) Ray Tang/Rex Features; 10 (t) Nils Jorgensen/Rex Features, (b) Northscot Press Agency/Rex Features; 11 (t) Charles M. Ommanney/Rex Features, (b) Greg Williams/Rex Features; 12 (t) David Bebber/Reuters; 13 (t) David Grey/Reuters; 14 (t) Action Press/Rex Features, (b) TDY/Rex Features; 16 (t) Stills Press Agency/Rex Features, 17 (b) Romeo Ranoco/Reuters; 22 (b) Nils Jorgensen/Rex Features; 23 (t/r) Stringer/Reuters, (b) Stringer/Reuters; 24 (c, b) SWS/Rex Features; 25 (t/r) Kimberly White/Reuters; 26 (t) Ken McKay/Rex Features, (b) Sipa Press/Rex Features; 27 (c/l) Peter Lomas/Rex Features; 28 (t) HO/Reuters; 29 (b) Phil Yeomans/Rex Features; 30 (t) Jennifer Podis/Rex Features, (b) Rex Features; 31 Mike Blake/Reuters; 32 (t) Patrick Barth/Rex Features, (b) Rex Features; 33 (b) David Hartley/Rex Features.

All other photos are from Ripley's Entertainment Inc.
Every attempt has been made to acknowledge correctly and contact copyright holders and we apologize in advance for any unintentional errors or omissions, which will be corrected in future editions.

Lincoln Township Public Library
2099 W. John Beers Rd.
Stevensville, MI 49127
(269) 429-9575